SOUTHERN · TIMES ·

Contents

. The next issue of Southern Times, No 8, will contain:
the LSWR C14 and S14 tank engines,
in and out of Works - colour images by **S C Townroe**,
more EMU's, and more Southern Region in colour.
Plus of course our other regular features,
, Treasures from the Bluebell Museum,
From the Footplate and as before, whatever else we can fit in!
We promise something for everyone.

The Transport Treasury

TIMES SERIES

Front Cover: Southern pull-push set No. 656 in the bay at Paddock Wood. *Gerald Daniels*

Above: On the automatically signalled section of line east of Basingstoke to Brookwood, new Battle of Britain pacific No. 21C155 as yet un-named, has been brought to a halt; the driver seen communicating with the signalman. Meanwhile a 'Mogul' passes on the opposite line. (See article on page 28.)

Rear cover: No. 34058 *Sir Frederick Pile* **waiting in the centre road at Exeter Central ready for the up 'Atlantic Coast Express'.**

Copies of many of the images within **SOUTHERN TIMES** are available for purchase / download.

In addition the Transport Treasury Archive contains tens of thousands of other UK, Irish and some European railway photographs.

© Kevin Robertson. Images (unless credited otherwise) and design The Transport Treasury 2023

ISBN 978-1-913251-60-4

First Published in 2023 by Transport Treasury Publishing Ltd., 16 Highworth Close, High Wycombe, HP13 7PJ

www.ttpublishing.co.uk or for editorial issues and contributions email to southerntimes@email.com

Printed in the Malta by the Gutenberg Press.

INTRODUCTION

Certainly not for the first time I find myself writing on a topic which is totally contrary to what is occurring outside.

On this occasion it happens to be the week commencing 4 September and for anyone with a slightly short memory this was the week when the mercury was north of 86 degrees (we still work in Fahrenheit here) and yet I had just completed the first article - turn over to page four and you will see what I mean.

At the same time we have been working hard on our first 'Southern Times - Extra' which should hit the shelves early in 2024. The subject is the 'Tavern Cars' something I have no doubt all will have heard of and which for our purposes started off life as an intended article for this issue - but then grew a bit. A visit to the National Archives also revealed an amount of new information plus an £80 fine on the way back for stopping with the back end of the car in a box junction, (these things happen;I knew I should have gone by train). However more is of course welcome, so if you have anything appropriate on the subject we would be delighted to hear from you.

I make no secret of my fascination for experiments that took place on the railway. The dilemma of course is does one spend time dwelling into such experiments or concentrate more on the every day scene? I hope a mixture of both is acceptable, my own rational being often experiments and unusual workings were by their very nature either one-off's or certainly not every day events and so justify inclusion. (As an example see the Kemp Town Civil Defence Exercise on page 42.)

In this issue I am pleased to say we can also achieve a bit of a catch-up. No that does not mean we are running short of material in any way - contributions of all types continue to be welcome - but we can at least include a good helping of 'From the Footplate' and the other articles promised from last time.

In this issue I have taken for the locomotive feature the subject of the N15X 4-6-0s. This small class of just seven engines did not last long enough to attract the preservationists and in many respects appear to have been overshadowed by the 'King Arthur' 4-6-0s; indeed their very class designation 'N15X' against 'N15' for the aforementioned confirms the type similarity.

However, today images of the N15X's appear only sporadically in the railway press and consequently it seemed only right it was time they received some more

detailed attention - exactly as per the T14 'Paddlebox' design featured in Issue 4.

Moving on, I am certainly no expert on the current heritage scene but I recall reading that certain current main line operators had to curtail their workings of late due to 'heritage' Mk1 stock not being fitted with remote locking. Apparently this does not apply on the heritage lines themselves as speeds are lower. I will not enter the debate although suffice to say I suppose it is a generational thing, travellers today used to being securely locked in their respective carriage. How on earth did we manage for all those years when we were responsible for our own safety?

Enough of my mutterings, I will conclude this deliberately shortened editorial with the accompanying attachment kindly send a little while ago by Graham Muspratt which I promised to use and now seems wholly appropriate for this time of year. Taking the suject of the poster quite literally, I expect I may even bump into some of you at Waterloo shortly; you will find me at the booking office window attempting to book a ticket for Torrington (or Padstow or Bude). Assuming of course we still have a booking office.....I had better not start off on that one!

Do remember though, if you would like to sound off on anything relating to our wonderful railway heritage and hopefully not too political, we always welcome guest editors. May I wish you all the compliments of the season and a happy and prosperous 2024.

Kevin Robertson

Remember the start of 1963 ?

Week after week of sub-zero temperatures with ice forming on top of already frozen snow. It seemed almost as soon as an area was cleared then it froze over again.

The railways were similarly badly hit, points and crossings regularly blocked with snow and signal wires freezing. In places electric trains could not leave their depots and so it was 'steam to the rescue'. Through it all the railways just got on with it and provided a service getting passengers and goods through when other forms of transport failed. The term 'the wrong type of snow' had not yet been heard although to be fair when it was there was some truth in those words; that is before they were hijacked by the media.

Perhaps surprisingly finding official factual information and illustrations on the workings of the time has proven extremely difficult and recourse has had to be made to sources such as the 'Railway Magazine'. In the April 1963 issue it reported, 'At Aldershot on January 3, steam locomotives were brought out to assist stranded local electric trains. Q1 No. 33035 and N 31811 were standing by in case of emergencies whilst Q No. 30548 passed through bearing a snow plough.' The same issue reported that the Q class were to be reduced to just seven examples and these will all be fitted with snow ploughs.

In the views seen here Roy Hobbs was at Redhill to record just a few examples of the weather albeit a few years earlier than 1963 - the coaches of the train being hauled by L1 No. 31775 looking none too inviting, likewise standard No. 76053 awaiting its next turn of duty.

Farnborough (Main). No. 34094 *Mortehoe* (left) and (below) an unidentified West Country on respective Down Bournemouth and Up West of England line services. In both case steam is not exactly being lifted clear of the engines although to be fair there would be a number of factors that could affect this; the speed, the cut-off and the actual weather conditions.

Opposite top: The regular Winchester City shunter No. 30096 likely out of steam (judging by the snow on the cylinders) and with some equally cold looking wagons in the yard behind. The almost 90° curve behind the engine explains why only short wheelbase locos were permitted here. *Larry Fullwood FS 34-2*

Opposite bottom: Still at Winchester and on the same day we find No. 30773 *Sir Lavaine* in its last days of working in charge of an Up van train - cold weather certainly affords an excellent steam effect. *Larry Fullwood FS 34-1*

Although, and as mentioned in the text, none of the N15X type survived long enough to attract the attention of the preservation movement, that is not to say they were totally ignored by the enthusiast fraternity. Here we see a Stephenson Locomotive Society special of 23 June 1956 with appropriately No. 32329 *Stephenson* taking the outward run of a tour from London Bridge to Brighton and seen emerging from Balcombe Tunnel at the head of its seven coach train. At Brighton there was a tour of the works with an optional extra trip over the Kemp Town branch for an additional 2/6d. On the return 'K' class 2-6-0 No. 32337 was in charge. *Horace Gamble*

The Southern N15X class

The Southern Railway N15X class owe their origins to the LBSCR 'L' class of 4-6-4T tank engines previously working on the Brighton main line.

Electrification of this route from 1 January 1933 rendered the class obsolete from their former duties although for a while afterwards similar work was available but with the engines now based at Eastbourne. Electrification though was spreading and after Eastbourne too was 'juiced' in 1935 there might have appeared to have been only one further opportunity for use on the Central Section and that was trains between Bognor and London - over what we might refer to as the Mid Sussex line.

Evidently such ideas had already been considered but also scuppered a few years earlier, for despite No. 328 (in its tank engine guise of course) having successfully worked services over this route in the winter of 1931/32, this has incurred the wrath of George Ellson, the Southern Chief Civil Engineer who refused to sanction the class for regular working over the drawbridge at Ford.

Ellson it will be recalled had been in charge as CCE at the time of the Sevonoaks disaster of a few years earlier (see articles in ST Nos 2 and 3) and would retain an aversion to large lank engines operating fast passenger services for the remainder of his career.

In consequence the Southern Railway was left with the dilemma as to what to do with seven large tank engines which in 1935 varied in age from 21 to just 13 years old.

Built to the more generous former LBSCR loading gauge, their very size prohibited their working elsewhere. Scrapping might then have been seen as the obvious solution except it will be recalled there already existed a precedent for the conversion of redundant tank engines into tender engines with the original 'U' class tender engines, the first batch of which had started life as the SECR 'K' class ('River') tanks. This rebuilding had begun in 1928.

According to Harry Holcroft in his biography 'Locomotive Adventure' (Ian Allan 1962) Holcroft had already proposed a scheme to convert the 'L' class tank engines into tender engines some years earlier in 1927. Holcroft does not elaborate further but it may

No 331 in charge of a Brighton line service in the period 1921 - 1922. Under 'LBSC' ownership the engine was un-named but upon rebuilding would become *Beattie*. The image was chosen as the physical size and height of the locomotive shows up well against the train which also has a Pullman car - which many Brighton line express services included - towards the rear. No 331 had been completed at Brighton works in December 1921.

No.	Name			New Number	Date renumbered	
327	*Charles C Macrae*	April 1914		2327	July 1932	Name removed July 1925
328		September 1914		2328	July 1933	
329	*Stephenson*	October 1921		2329	July 1932	
330		December 1921		2330	April 1933	
331		December 1921		2331`	May 1933	
332		March 1922		2332	April 1933	
333	*Remembrance*	April 1922		2333	November 1932	

Top: Last of the class, and one of the two that would retain its name, *Remembrance* when new outside Brighton Works. The painted name was replaced by a cast plate under Southern Railway ownership in May 1927. The plate attached under the name reads 'In grateful remembrance of the 532 men of the LB&SCR Rly. who gave their lives for their country 1914-1919.' The engine is painted in 'Photographic grey' and it will be noted the rods are positioned 'down' so likely deliberate. Other images from the time show either this or another member of the class with a 'Terrier' so affording a 'little and large' comparison.

Bottom: Bradley refers an unfortunate incident - but without an accompanying illustration - at Brighton at 12 55 pm on 30 September 1922 when No. 329 *Stephenson* continued over the turntable and through a brick wall injuring a pedestrian. Driver John Yates was found to have omitted to move a superheated engine within the shed confines without having the cylinder cocks open, hence even though the regulator was closed the engine continued on its way. He was duly censured. This particular engine had a reputation for erratic steaming and in consequence in June of the next year was fitted with Trick valves whilst the lap distance was increased and the lead reduced. Steaming was improved but at the cost of more fire being thrown from the chimney, a greater accumulation of ash in the smokebox and consequent warping of the smokebox door. Further changes saw an alteration to the diameter of the blast pipe which resulted in improved coal consumption compared with the rest of the class. Even so it is not certain if similar changes were applied to other class members.

Our final view of one of the class in tank engine form, No. 329 again but this with a cast Southern nameplate and the 'B' prefix above the number. (The un-named members of the class had their number on the bunker side.) Various changes were made to the design in Southern days including improved side control first on the front and then later on the trailing bogie. Vacuum ejectors and the provision for steam heating at the front end and the removal of the cylinder tail-rods were further changes. (No. 327 had been named after the then Chairman of the LBSCR, Charles C Macrae.)

well have coincided with the introduction of King Arthur class engines on the same services.

In the event rebuilding was the course of action decided upon and this before electrification to Eastbourne had commenced. Accordingly No. 2329 *Stephenson* was taken into Eastleigh Works for rebuilding on 12 July 1934. As an example of the different loading gauge criteria applicable between the Brighton and South Western lines, the cab roof, safety-vale casing, dome

cover and chimney all had to be removed before No. 2329 could travel west.

Retaining its same number, No. 2329 emerged replete as a tender engine on 6 December 1934. In this revised form it was attached to a double bogie tender from an S15 carrying 5,000 gallons of water and 3 tons of coal. The tender was also fitted with additional vacuum cylinders on the top behind the coal space whilst footsteps and handrails were provided at the rear.

No.	To Eastleigh	To traffic as 4-6-0	Time spend in works (complete months)	Tender from S15 No.	Loco name
2327	17-11-1934	4-4-1935	4+	509	*Trevethick*
2328	3-9-1935	1-2-1936	4+	505	*Hackworth*
2329	12-7-1934	6-12-1934	4+	833	*Stephenson*
2330	25-3-1935	18-9-1935	5+	507	*Cudworth*
2331`	30-12-1935	11-4-1936	3+	504	*Beattie*
2332	12-7-1935	9-11-1935	2+	510	*Stroudley*
2333	7-12-1935	27-6-1935	6+	506	Remembrance

No. 2332 *Stroudley* in steam within the confines of Nine Elms shed. Again likely soon after rebuilding as witness the unblemished livery. Of note are the provision of snifting valves and the lining on the front foot steps. The original oval buffers from tank engine days were retained although at the opposite end the tender buffers were of the more conventional circular type. The engine also retains the large guard irons that were a feature of LBSCR designs.

Seen from the rear at Waterloo. No. 2329 presents an equally impressive appearance heightened perhaps by the provision of the vacuum reservoirs on the tender, The engine was working Nine Elms duty No. 20 and having been relieved of its train will likely now reverse to Loco Junction ready to drop down on to the shed for servicing.

Archived%20pages/SLS_nameplates_etc.htm.) With the exception of *Remembrance* all the names also had cast 'Remembrance Class' into the lower half of the plate.

It should be mentioned that as electrification progressed in Sussex so further cascading of motive power took place. A total of 14 King Arthur class engines subsequently moving east to work on the Kent Coast lines.

Back on the Western section, Nine Elms first used the N15X type on a variety of top link duties, according to Bradley these mainly involved Bournemouth and Portsmouth line turns. They might also be seen at the head of a Waterloo - Southampton Docks working in place of the more usual H15. Bradley adds, 'Very occasionally one headed the 'Bournemouth Belle' and less frequently the West of England services.' The latter comment is slightly at odds with Holcroft who notes, '...a duty on which they excelled was the operation of milk trains for the West Country.'

As rebuilds they were handsome engines with a well proportioned external appearance. In service they were noted for a having a crisp exhaust, but sight and sound were not all and compared with a 'King Arthur' the N15X type were considered less capable.

Top: No. 2328 *Hackworth,* this image clearly showing the position of the left hand clack box. The total weight of engine and tender in working order was 130t 13cwt, the tender amounting for 57t 11cwt including 5 tons of coal and 5,000 gallons of water. It is not believed any form of water treatment was ever fitted.

Bottom: No. 2332 *Stroudley* at Bournemouth Central in May 1947 after arriving with an inter-company working. This engine was then in malachite green; a table of livery changes shown below. From rebuilding up to 1941 all repaints had been in Southern livery. *Thomas Rendell / Transport Treasury*

Notes on liveries:

At the time of rebuilding all engines were turned out in the then standard SR livery of dark green with black frames and black and white lining, lettering was in yellow (see illustration page 14).
'Bulleid livery' consisted Maunsell dark green, black and white lining, black cylinders and smoke deflectors and cab side numbers.
'Olive green' was an olive green with black and yellow lining, black cylinders and the top half of the smoke deflectors in green with the lower half black.
Repaints after February 1941 were in plain black.

No.	Bulleid livery	Olive green	SR Malachite	BR Malachite	BR lined black		
2327		May 1940	Jul 1946		Apr 1950		
2328				Oct 1948	Apr 1951		
2329		Feb 1940	Nov 1947		Apr 1950	May 1952	Sep 1954
2330		Aug 1939		Feb 1948	Oct 1951		
2331			Nov 1947		Jan 1953		
2332		No 1939	May 1946	May 1948	Feb 1952	Apr 1954	
2333	Feb 1939		Feb 1947	Apr 1949	Apr 1952		

No. 2328 at Eastleigh in June 1948 and still wearing wartime plain black. It would be repainted in malachite green and receive its BR number four months later. The engine is on a Portsmouth service formed of LSWR stock.

Accordingly it was not long before they were relegated to the 'second division' in charge of semi-fast, Saturday relief and excursions trains; the type of passenger work an H15, S15, or Paddlebox might otherwise have been called upon to take (for detail on the latter, see issue 4 of 'ST').

This comment might appear slightly strange as whilst working in original form Bradley makes no comment on adverse performance. Indeed in a series of trails in January 1927 No. 331 running in original tank engine form had returned the best coal consumption figures when compared against a former SECR 'K' class tank, Brighton 'Atlantic' No. 425 and 'King Arthur' No. E803. Accordibngly it is difficuelt to see how this might have changed upon rebuilding.

It was this indifferent performance, notwithstanding some of the redesigned engines having little more than two years in rebuilt service, that the new Southern Railway CME Mr Bulleid decided to investigate.

Thus in October 1938 after just one year in office, the new CME ordered a series of trials (we are not told which engine was involved) in an attempt to establish why boiler pressure might drop from the maximum working pressure of 180lbs to perhaps 110-125psi when working between Clapham Junction and Basingstoke, this with just with eight coaches and on a normal express schedule. At the same time cost of maintenance both on shed and at works were considered.

Such investigation might well have concluded the type were not worthy of further development but we should also consider the political stage at the time and it may well have been that owing to their recent (re)build it was felt their retention should be considered in what were increasingly uncertain times.

The conclusion from the tests was that by opening up the cylinder ports, shortening the blast pipe and modifying the brick arch improvement could be achieved and engines were subsequently modified as they entered works for overhaul. All seven being dealt with between February 1939 and September 1940.

Bradley now makes for an unusual and slightly contradictory comment for he states, 'Some improvement was noticeable, but the Urie and Maunsell 'King Arthurs' were still more versatile as well as being lighter on fuel and maintenance.' This was the last attempt at modifications for the type and all seven engines would continue in a secondary role for the remainder of their lives.

The start of WW2 saw the immediate curtailment of some of the services they had previously worked, although evacuation trains and military / government workings meant they continued to be useful. Following this initial peak matters quietened and with now little extra or excursion work required, by Christmas 1939 four were laid up our of use at Nine Elms with the remaining three spending more time on shed than at work. All however were in use leading up to Dunkirk,

No. 2331 *Beattie* taking a special train of men from an anti-aircraft regiment to Tonbridge in the early hours of 28 May. Here the defence force was set up and ready for action by mid morning although the placing of two Bofors guns at the London end of the platform had necessitated the removal of the engine water column - this omission made good thanks to the local fire brigade. The same engine was later used that morning to pilot a D1 4-4-0 on a troop train heading towards Redhill.

The class were then kept busy for the rest of the summer of 1940 but after which and into the autumn / winter only two or three might be occupied and just on local goods or shunting duties in the London area. This might seem strange as an engine with driving wheels of 6' 9" diameter would ordinarily hardly be considered suitable for such a turn.

Their use - if at all - for most of 1941 is not reported until that is November 1941 when a request was made by the GWR for urgent motive power, the initial response from the SR being to send two of the class

together with four S15's a pair of I3's. Meanwhile four more N15x members were sent to Eastleigh to be prepared for loan. (No. 2333 does not appear to feature in Bradley's notes so we cannot be certain if it too was loaned out.) Possibly this shortfall in GWR motive power came about with the requisitioning of 100 Dean Goods engines both for service abroad and also at military depots in the UK.

In official GWR parlance, the N15X was given a 'Red' route availability and placed in the same load haulage capacity as that of a GWR 2-cylinder 'Saint'.

Bradley reports the movement / work of several members of the class at different times; No. 2329 at Newton Abbot in the early months of 1942 and noted as frequently working an early morning passenger train to Exeter, the same engine having formally been based at Exeter. Nos. 2327 and 2330 were at Old Oak Common, No. 2331 at Swindon and No. 2332 at Gloucester. Apart from the example of 2329, most of their work appears to have been on goods or van trains. No mention appears to be made of No. 2333 although

Above: A mixture of liveries for No. 32327 *Trevethick*; Southern malachite on the engine, including the smoke deflectors, and also the tender but with 'British Railways' on the tender (the time before an emblem have been finalised.)

Opposite top: The elusive one! No. 32330 *Cudworth* which appears only rarely in photographs of the time. It is seen here ambling along past Barton Mill carriage sidings just east of Basingstoke and hardly likely to be earning its keep.

Opposite bottom - Waterloo - Basingstoke duty for No. 32331 *Beattie.* This was a regular duty for the class. A poor quality view of the same engine taken in 1955 at Basingstoke shows the attached tender still displaying the word 'Southern' although the engine is in (dirty) plain black. Unfortunately the quality of the view makes it impossible to determine if it is a black engine with a green tender. We have no details if tender swaps occurred as engine passed through works.

Opposite top: No. 32329 - seemingly the most regularly photographed member of the class - on ECS shunting duty at the east end of Basingstoke station and opposite the down line.

Opposite bottom: Similar mundane duty except this time it is goods stock, for No. 32331 at Farnborough. As per Holcroft's earlier comment, and despite not being mentioned as a specific duty on page 25, we know the class were also active on milk trains into the 1950s.

Above: Queens Road on the 5.09pm Waterloo - Basingstoke, 27 July 1950. In the background is the Hampton & Sons storage repository immediately before which it was just possible to gain a very quick glimpse down at Stewarts Lane depot. *Peter Pescod / Transport* Treasury.

it certainly was transferred as former Didcot Fireman Harold Gasson in his published reminiscences refers to a positive experience working on this engine in 1942. (Harold and his mate had taken over from another crew on No. 2333 the fireman having complained the engine was shy for steam. This was confirmed by an inspector who was riding with them. Harold had previously seen one of the class at Eastleigh where a friendly Southern fireman had explained how they would steam if fired 'all over the box'. Harold did this and with considerable improvement to the performance of No. 2333.)

Whilst on loan, two of the class, Nos. 2331 and 2332 were repaired at Swindon (twice for No. 2331) but others were returned to Eastleigh when necessary. No. 2328 was sent back to Eastleigh for a change of boiler and new cylinders, a repair that in the event took so long it was never did return to the GWR. All were back

on Southern metals by July 1943, their place on the GWR now taken by newly built Stanier 2-8-0s erected at Swindon.

Evidently No. 2333's time on the GWR had not been long for with the return of the remaining engines to Nine Elms and according to the Nine Elms foreman in far better order than might have been expected, No. 2333 at last could be despatched to Eastleigh for long overdue repairs - evidently any movement had been heralded with various rumblings and thumps, its steaming capabilities similarly somewhat erratic.

History would now start to repeat itself, for whilst 15 or so years ago as tank engines the L class had been rendered redundant from Brighton, now with the influx of large numbers of new Bulleid pacifics, so the N15X type would be similarly redundant from Nine Elms. In

Above: No. 32329 again, but this time at Reading WR shed 26 June 1955 and unusually carrying the Southern Region route code disc for Waterloo - Basingstoke. The class were semi-regular performers on the inter-regional trains running via Reading although usually engines on these services were exchanged at Oxford.

Opposite top: No. 32331 receiving attention inside Eastleigh Works.

Opposite bottom: No. 32329 outside the main office block at Eastleigh shed. Most engines would be facing in the opposite direction at this point hence by inference No 32329 has either arrived from the Portsmouth or Southampton direction and come off its train to reverse into the shed.

consequence all seven were transferred to Basingstoke in turn replacing U class 2-6-0 engines.

From Basingstoke they worked to Waterloo, Reading and Portsmouth but might also occasionally venture as far as Salisbury. The engines could also be seen on through trains off the Great Western - later the Western Region. As none of these tasks were particularly taxing so wear was minimised and in what was to be their final years several achieved high mileages between repairs.

Having dodged the scrap man 20 years earlier they would not be so lucky now. In addition to the large number of Bulleid types now working, the Southern Region had started to receive 76xxx, 75xxx and 73xxx types. It was then hardly surprising when all seven engines were included in the current withdrawal programme.

First to go was No 32328 sent to Eastleigh with cracked frames and a weak firebox crown in January 1955. It was followed by No 32330 in August of the same year.

Four were condemned in 1956, Nos. 32327 along with 32332 in January, No 32333 in April and No. 32329 in July. The last, No. 32331 would outlive its compatriots by a year and survived until July 1957.

No. 32333 was scheduled to be broken up at Brighton (did it arrive there under its own steam?) and after arrival for breaking on 4 April was thoroughly cleaned and on 10 April in company with the last R1 0-6-0T No. 31704 taken to Lovers Walk to be photographed. One set of nameplates and plaques was removed from No. 32333 and displayed at the entrance to the offices at the works. Upon the closure of the works, their subsequent

Opposite page: Opposites indeed. Top we have No. 32329 *Stephenson* neatly turned out and receiving deserved glances at Brighton having arrived with the SLS special of 23 June 1956. Below we see the sad remains of No. 32327 *Trevithick* at Eastleigh after the Woking accident of 23 December 1955.

Above: No 32328 formerly carrying *Hackworth* nameplates on the scrap line at Eastleigh. It has lost its original tender and is now temporarily attached to a Drummond water cart ex S15 No.30509 which will be scrapped at the same time as the engine.

fate is not reported.

The end for No. 32327 had been ignominious to say the least for on 23 December 1955 it was involved in a rear end collision near Woking whilst hauling the 7.50 pm Waterloo - Basingstoke service, colliding with the rear of the preceding 7.45 pm Waterloo - Portsmouth electric service. Notwithstanding the impact and the speed being at the most 10mph, there was severe damage to the front of the engine but fortunately no serious injuries although debris from the collision struck a passing Up Bournemouth service. Cautiously towed to Eastleigh, repair was hardly likely to be considered and the engine was officially withdrawn a few weeks later. (The official accident report is available at https://www.railwaysarchive.co.uk/documents/MoT_Woking1955.pdf .)

No. 32329 had also worked two special trains in its last weeks, the previously mentioned SLS tour of 23 June and then on its last day in traffic, 8 July 1956, the final leg of the RCTS 'Wessex Wyvern' tour from Andover to Waterloo. This was handled in style, with a maximum of 80mph before a signal check at Hampton Court Junction; the society headboard disappearing from the front of the engine in the process!

Other than the usual checks on the engine before any day's work, it is not thought any special preparation had been made to No. 32329 hence there was some doubt as to the accuracy of its call to scrap when it reached Brighton just four days later on 12 July, it would not survive.

The final member of the class, No. 32331, had also been at Brighton in the same month, this time not for scrap but instead for minor repairs after which it returned to Basingstoke. With two of the class at Brighton and No. 32331 already reportedly as 'rough', might it not have made sense to effect a substitution and grant a reprieve to No.3232? Common sense on the ground perhaps but then the number crunchers had already spoken and there was no reprieve.

Returning to Basingstoke for the very last time, No. 32331 was rostered on trains to Portsmouth, the through Bournemouth service from Newcastle and

No. 32331, formerly *Beattie*, at the rear of Eastleigh works on 25 August 1957 just one month after withdrawal and clearly not long for this world. The nameplates have been removed; perhaps the smokebox plate would be salvaged once cutting commenced. Alongside Standard Class 4 No. 76027 would survive until October 1965 and was seen here probably parked pending repair / overhaul. It would have a working life of just 12 years compared with the 36 for No.32331, 21 of that being as a 4-6-0.
R C Riley / Transport Treasury

an evening freight to Oxford. A highlight came on 3 November when it replaced failed No. 35022 on a Bournemouth - Waterloo working. For its final months it was mostly employed on light freight turns with a last horah on 23 June 1957 when it took a return trip from London Bridge to Windsor & Eton Riverside and return.

Duties.

Official Allocations / Engine Workings for the Summer of 1954 show all seven of the class allocated to Basingstoke (70D) throughout the BR period. With the exception of No 32331 all of the class are also shown stored at various times either for several weeks or even a few months and at different periods throughout the year. The location of storage is not shown but would depend on available space; This would either be at Basingstoke or Eastleigh.

The 1954 Summer workings show four engines required on a daily basis;

Duty 231 - Shunting and then a return trip to Waterloo On Saturday only the loco would finish its turn at Salisbury.

Duty 233 - Single return trip to Waterloo having taken over the 9.02 am from Bournemouth. On Saturday loco worked light to Reading (WR loco) thence a train to Portsmouth and return to Basingstoke. Saturdays 17 July to 28 August would have the engine take over the 10.30 pm ex Mansfield at Basingstoke at 3.05 am and work through to Bournemouth West, returning with a morning passenger train from Bournemouth Central to Basingstoke.

Duty 236 - Weekdays, passenger working between Basingstoke and Reading, two round trips. Except on Monday the engine on this turn would also take the 3.20 am 'Papers' from Waterloo as far as Basingstoke. The second Reading trip would see the loco continue to Eastleigh and then take the 7.55pm ex Bournemouth West as far as Basingstoke.

Duty 238 - Basingstoke to Reading including shunting at Reading between 12.00 pm and 1.30 pm followed by a train to Portsmouth and return to Basingstoke. Saturday only the extension to Portsmouth was replaced by a freight duty from Basingstoke to Banbury returning light engine.

Details for Sundays are not available.

	BR Number	Withdrawn	Scrapped at	Mileage	Tender to No / date
32327	Jul 1949	Jan 1956	Eastleigh	1,210,,802	
32328	Oct 1948	Jan 1955	Eastleigh *	1,048,374	30509 / Feb 1955
32329	Dec 1948	Jul 1956	Brighton	1,119,528	30508 / Nov 1956
32330	Aug 1948	Aug 1955		1,016,543	
32331	May 1949	Sep 1957		1,008, 431 (491,064 in tank form)	30806 / Aug 1958
32332	May 1949	Jan 1956		1,066,737	
32333	May 1948	Apr 1956		1,045,001	30451 / Feb 1957

No 32328 had been due to be towed to Brighton for scrap but due to a strike of loco crews was instead dealt with at Eastleigh.

The end for No. 32328 outside the rear of Eastleigh Works.

The end finally came a few weeks later in July 1957.

Note: Readers may recall I touched briefly upon the technical revolution that Artificial Intelligence may bring in the future including perhaps to railway research. As an experiment I asked an AI Bot what it could tell me on the N15X class of engine, the results were 'interesting'. An initial description was concise and accurate but reading on, AI Bot clearly became confused as what it provided next was - and I quote:

"Here are some of the notable members of the N15X class: No. 30778 Brunel: This locomotive was named after Isambard Kingdom Brunel, the famous British engineer. It was the last N15X locomotive to be built. No. 30780 Stephenson: This locomotive was named after George Stephenson, the father of the railways. It was one of the first N15X locomotives to be built." Elsewhere on the internet it is also mentioned one example of an N15X is preserved.

This is mentioned purely as a cautionary tale as clearly AI Bot picked this up by scouring the internet, which is of course where it obtains its information. The sources used for this article are principally Bradley and the 'R.O'.

A few years ago there was the term, 'The camera cannot lie' - but it certainly can nowadays with the ability to manipulate images into things that never actually existed or appeared - we do NOT do this in Southern Times. Similarly we have today the modern equivalent 'If it is on the

Just as we were going to press a new source of information on the class revealed itself. This new information will be incorporated in a supplementary article on the N15X class to appear in Issue 8.

Signalling at Farnborough Main
Based on notes by the late John Davenport

In 1950 I was fortunate to be issued with a line-side photography pass by the Southern Region, covering the section from Farnborough Main to Worting Junction, west of Basingstoke. I was told that contact should be made with a railway employee before walking off the end of the platform - it saved the despatch of a posse to bring you back - and the obvious place to go was the signal box. So on my first visit to Farnborough I went to the box at the end of the down platform. It turned out to be the first of many visits.

Because the London and South Western Railway had been a pioneer in automatic signalling, the box did not have the normal row of tall levers projecting from a metal frame on the floor. Instead there was a big wooden cabinet, from the front of which protruded, just about waist high, a row of handles about four inches high at the end of horizontal slides. The handles had different colours for signals and points and a movement in and out of about four inches. Above them, on the top of the cabinet, were two bells with tappers at each end of the cabinet for communicating with the signal boxes on either side, one for the through lines and the other for the local lines. Hanging above and at the back of the cabinet was the track diagram of the area controlled by the box with two red lights for each section of track occupied by a train. The diagram was of the "normally dark" type, with a small green light, permanently lit, mounted at the top of the frame.
This green light was installed after a collision on 26 November, 1947, three miles west of the box. There had been a power failure due to the main fuse blowing in Stud Lane substation, which meant that no signals would work, nor did any train light up the track diagram. Unfortunately the 3.5pm from Bournemouth West had been stopped on the Up through opposite Cove Camp at an automatic signal which would not clear. The driver was unable to make contact by 'phone with the Farnborough signalman, whilst there was also something of a panic between Fleet box, which had just been switched in, Farnborough and Brookwood. In all this, the Bournemouth train remained invisible. The following fast line train, the 12.15 from Ilfracombe, was allowed to leave Fleet under caution to reach Farnborough and report that the line was clear. Regrettably it was not, and No 453 *King Arthur* hit the back of the Bournemouth train at about 20 mph sadly resulting with two fatalities.

One of the recommendations in the Inspecting Officer's Report was that a "Power on" light should be provided so that signalmen would be aware of failure and take action.

The Farnborough frame had 40 slides, including two blue "King Levers" (Nos 1 and 31) which switched the signals to automatic when the box was closed. In reality this lever had not been used since 1939, the box open 24/7 initial because of the build-up of military traffic.

Seen from an approaching Waterloo bound train on 24 August 1959, this is Farnborough station with the pneumatic signal box on the right facing the down slow line. *Henry Priestley / Transport Treasury*

The up starting signals at Farnborough. The system was in many respects similar to what would later be modern day MAS with full track circuiting, the presence of a train resetting the signal in the rear to 'on' (danger). What it could not do however, was automatically alter the line the train was running on, hence if the signalman required an up service on the slow line to crossover and join the up through line then manual intervention was required. *Adrian Swain / Transport Treasury*

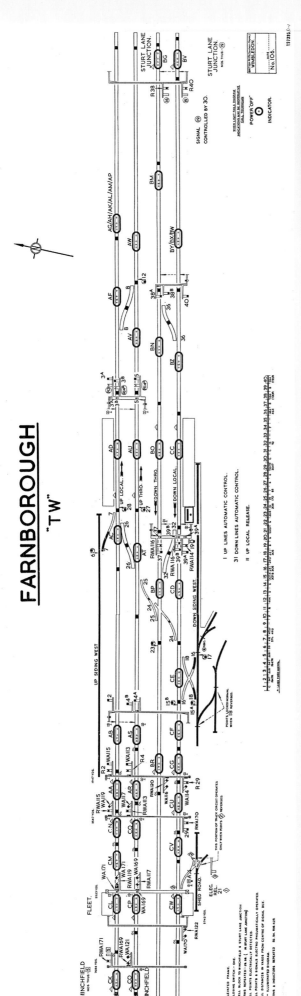

D15 4-4-0 No. 30465 leaving Farnborough on a down Basingstoke service. The presence of track circuit 'CD' immediately in advance of the starting signal No 39A, has restored the signal to 'On' notwithstanding the fact part of the train is still occupying track 'CC'. The occupied track circuits also prevent the signalman altering the position of any crossover directly affected by the two track circuits mentioned, viz Nos 32 and 24. *John Davenport / Transport Treasury*

The South Western had sent an investigatory party to the United States around 1900, and as a result had introduced this signalling system which was both automatic and also track circuit controlled. It was at first operated by low pressure pneumatic power, later converted to electro pneumatic. It eventually extended continuously from west of Woking to Basingstoke. Its distinguishing feature outside station areas being the gantries spanning all four tracks. These gantries were spaced about a mile apart. Each track had a stop signal set above a distant signal, which was effectively a repeater for the stop signal in advance.

Because the track circuits controlled not only the automatic gantry signals but also the ability to operate any lever in the frame, there were no block instruments, only the bells to the next boxes. East of Farnborough, Sturt Lane Junction was only switched in when trains were crossing to or from the main lines for the Ascot Branch, hence Brookwood was the usual box in contact. When a down passenger train passed Brookwood, the signalman there would give one beat - "Call attention" - on the appropriate bell, through or local line, which like all bell signals had to be repeated by the receiving signalman as acknowledgement. Brookwood would then send "Three pause One" on say the through line, again acknowledged. This meant a passenger train was coming. If the tracks were clear at Farnborough, the two slides for the down through signals would be pulled out, giving the train a clear road to a mile short of Fleet. The diagram would light up as the train reached the limit of the tracks shown, and the slides would replace themselves as the appropriate track circuit was reached. The man at Farnborough would repeat the sequence of bell signals to Fleet as the train passed his box. With this system, no "Train out of Section" code was sent to Brookwood.

One of those odd historical quirks applied to Farnborough even if its actual application was some few miles further west; this was that it was necessary to know whether a train was

As referred to in the text, John was present at Farnborough on a number of occasions to record the train service. This is his log for Saturday 12 July 1952 from 2.30 pm to 7.08 pm.

2.20 pm	Down Main	1.22 pm	Waterloo - Bournemouth	No. 30864	
2.24 pm	Down Main	1.30 pm	Waterloo - Weymouth	No.34104	
2.25 pm	Up Main	11.02 am	Weymouth - Waterloo	No. 34043	Noted with new tender
2.29 pm	Up Main	11.30 am	Weymouth - Waterloo	No. 10202	
2.38 pm	Up Main	09.20 am	Torrington - Waterloo	No. 32327	
2.38 pm	Down Local	1.24 pm	Waterloo - Salisbury	No. 30512	
2.44 pm	Up Main	08.05 am	Wadebridge - Waterloo	No. 30450	
2.49 pm	Up Local	12.58 pm	Salisbury - Waterloo	No. 35012	Noted with new tender
2.55 pm	Up Main	10.00 am	Mortehoe - Waterloo	No. 34009	
2.55 pm	Down Main	2.00 pm	Waterloo - So'ton Docks	No. 34045	
2.59 pm	Up Main	11.45 am	Weymouth - Waterloo		Loco not recorded
3.05 pm	Down Local	1.45 pm	Waterloo - Bulford	No. 31621	Military
3.11 pm	Up Main	1.11 pm	Portsmouth - Colne	No. 34007	Lancashire
3.16 pm	Up Main	08.30 am	Padstow - Waterloo	No. 35025	
3.21 pm	Down Local	2.53 pm	Woking -Basingstoke	No. 33002	Goods
3.31 pm	Up Local	11.48 am	Bournemouth - Woking	No. 30920	

Continued overleaf

No. 30852 *Sir Walter Raleigh* on the Up Main approaching Farnborough with a Waterloo boat train; note a Pullman car is just visible in the formation. Again the track circuit ahead of the home signal 'AT' has restored the arm, No 4A, to danger. On the down line gantry it will be noted there are co-acting arms provided. *Hugh Davies / Transport Treasury* .

3.32 pm	Up Main	10.30 am	Ilfracombe - Waterloo	No. 35008	'ACE'
3.34 pm	Down Main	2.30 pm	Waterloo - Weymouth	No. 30789	
3.39 pm	Down Main	2.34 pm	Waterloo - Bournemouth	No. 30865	
3.43 pm	Up Main	1.25 pm	Lymington - Waterloo	No. 31917	
3.49 pm	Up Main	1.05 pm	Bournemouth - Waterloo	No.34010	
3.53 pm	Down Main	3.00 pm	Waterloo - Ilfracombe	No. 34004	
3.56 pm	Up Main	12.20 pm	Weymouth - Waterloo	No. 30783	
3.57 pm	Down Local	2.54 pm	Waterloo - Basingstoke	No. 30826l	
3.57 pm	Down Main	3.05 pm	Waterloo - Exeter	No. 35024	
4.00 pm	Up Main	1.45 pm	Bournemouth - Waterloo	No. 30860	
4.03 pm	Down Main	3.30 pm	Waterloo -Bournemouth	No. 30861	
4.04 pm	Up Main	2.50 pm	So'ton Docks - Waterloo	No. 32328	
4.11 pm	Up Main	10.40 am	Torrington - Waterloo	No. 34063	
4.15 pm	Down Main	3.06 pm	Waterloo - Farnborough	No. 34110	Empties to local then yard
4.24 pm	Down Local		F'borough - Basingstoke	No. 34110	Light engine
4.25 pm	Up Main	11.30 am	Ilfracombe - Waterloo	No. 35023	
4.30 pm	Down Main	3.30 pm	Waterloo- Bournemouth	No. 30863	
4.38 pm	Up Main	2.10 pm	Bournemouth - Waterloo	No. 30747	
4.41 pm	Up Local	2.47 pm	Salisbury - Waterloo	No. 30449	
4.43 pm	Up Main	1.33 pm	Swanage - Waterloo	No. 34093	Checked
4.45 pm	Up Main	12.00 pm	Ilfracombe - Waterloo	No. 35017	'Devon Belle' - checked
4.52 pm	Up Main	3.25 pm	So'ton Docks - Waterloo	No. 30744	
4.52 pm	Down Main	4.00 pm	Waterloo - So'ton Docks	No. 30742	
4.53 pm	Down Local	3.54 pm	Waterloo - Basingstoke	No. 30745	
5.02 pm	Down main	4.04 pm	Waterloo - Marchwood	No. 30839	
5.02 pm	Up Main	1.25 pm	Weymouth - Waterloo	No. 30749	
5.05 pm	Up Local	3.51 pm	So'ton Docks - Waterloo	No. 30739	
5.06 pm	Down Local	3.54 pm	Clapham Yard - Yeovil	No. 30483	Empty milk tanks
5.06 pm	Up Main	10.45 am	Padstow - Waterloo	No. 35006	
5.10 pm	Up Local	3.58 pm	So'ton Docks - Waterloo	No. 30853	
5.19 pm	Down Main	4.35 pm	Waterloo - Weymouth	No. 10202	'Royal Wessex'
5.21 pm	Up Local		Basingstoke - Guildford	No. 33002	Light engine
5.32 pm	Down Main	4.22 pm	Waterloo - Bournemouth	No. 30748	
5.35 pm	Up Main	3.40 pm	Lymington Pier - Waterloo	No. 31909	
5.41 pm	Up Main	4.23 pm	So'ton Docks - Waterloo	No. 30850	
5.47 pm	Down Main	5.02 pm	Waterloo - Exeter	No. 35001	
5.50 pm	Up Main	2.58 pm	Seaton - Waterloo	No. 30457	
5.56 pm	Up Main	3.12 pm	Bournemouth Waterloo	No. 35005	
6.00 pm	Up Main	11.35 am	Plymouth - Waterloo	No. 35014	
6.02 pm	Down Local	4.54 pm	Waterloo - Ludgershall	No. 31633	
6.08 pm	Up Main	4.55 pm	So'ton Docks - Waterloo	No. 30910	
6.09 pm	Up Local	4.15 pm	Salisbury - Waterloo	No. 30484	
6.13 pm	Down Main	5.00 pm	Waterloo - Weymouth	No. 30856	
6.18 pm	Up Main	4.34 pm	Bournemouth - Waterloo	No. 35021	Noted with new tender

for Southampton or Salisbury. The original line of the 1830s had been the London and Southampton Railway, so that route was referred to as the main line and a passenger train for that route would be sent on as "Three pause One". It was Farnborough's job to "turn the code" for the Salisbury line, which was treated as the Branch line, thus for example, the Atlantic Coast Express would be received as "Three pause One" and sent on as "One pause Three". Note; the usual code for an express passenger was of course four beats, but this could not turned, hence all passenger workings were 'three pause one'. The signalman was also expected to confirm his decision by observation of the engine headcode; the Southern's use of 'route' codes theoretically making this task straightforward – except

that it is at night – although the headlamps should be lit -, in fog, when the engine was obscured by another train etc etc.

At the time of installation, which coincided with the completion of the quadrupling of the line between Woking and Worting Junction, the signally system was technically very advanced and it continued to work well fifty years on. It was also very flexible - on a Sunday afternoon in winter the next box open westwards from Farnborough was Basingstoke East, and all signals between there and Farnborough were working automatically although It took a long time for an up train to appear on the diagram after the bell code had been received, and even longer for an all-stations stopper.

Equally the signalling coped with heavy traffic on summer Saturdays. On 12 July 1952, between 2.20 pm 7.08 pm the box dealt with 67 trains, or one every 4.3 minutes. These were routed 10 on the down local, 16 on the down through, 33 on the up through and 8 on the up local. On 26 July, the morning produced 41 trains between 9:48 am and 12.38 pm - 6 on the down local, 18 on the down through, 13 on the up through and 4 on the up local. The average was one every 4.1

minutes. As each one had to be entered on the booking sheets as well as dealt with by bells and slides, it was a busy time.

The system lasted until the Bournemouth electrification in the mid 1960's, creaking a bit towards the end, but a tribute to the engineers of sixty years earlier.

Gantry between Fleet and Farnborough 16 April 1960. Reference to the signal diagram will show this to be the next gantry immediately west of Farnborough. *Hugh Davies / Transport Treasury*

John Davenport's notes include observations and illustrations on Farnborough Air Show traffic in the early 1950s. It is our intention to include these in a future issue.

Down the line to Oxted: Part 2
Alan Postlethwaite

Station buildings on the Oxted line were in SER style - single storey brick with tall chimney stacks and generous canopies.
At Oxted, the Down bay on the right was used for push-pull services to Tunbridge Wells West via Hever. After arrival in the Up platform, this push-pull train has pulled forward and is reversing onto the Down line to reach the bay. The 'barley sugar' lamp post and Sugg Rochester gas lamps are early SR patterns. The man on the right is wearing the standard commuting kit of bowler, raincoat, briefcase and 'Daily Telegraph'.

All change at Oxted! Maunsell brake composite No. 6681 was built in 1935. A pull-push cab was added in 1959 and Set 602 was scrapped in 1963. Its front windows are much smaller than those on push-pull conversions of pre-Grouping stock. They are similar to those of the new green DEMU No. 1311 seen arriving from Victoria. *Alan Postlethwaite, 1963.*

Filling the tanks at Oxted while the signalman chats to the driver of class 4MT tank No. 80032. The buildings on this joint line were SER but the signal boxes were LBSCR. *Alan Postlethwaite, 1962.*

Framed by a skyline silhouette of winter trees, class 4MT tank No. 80089 bursts forth from the west portal of Limpsfield tunnel. Note how the low sunshine brings out the texture of the grass, plume and locomotive. This class was elegant and modernistic with interesting outside motion. It somehow blended with the clean lines of Bulleid coaches, a perfect match.

Oxted's Up distant signal helps to frame class H tank No. 31544 heading a pull-push service from the Hever line. It is the setting of the trees and grassy cutting, however, that make this scene beautiful.

Pull-push set No. 659 restarts from Hurst Green's Down home signals. The far distant arm is on its way up to 'clear' for the Hever line. The coaches are ex-SECR, enhanced by the tall windows of the pull push cab. Currently, EMUs from London Bridge run via Hever to Uckfield. We might alight at Eridge on to a preserved steam train of the Spa Valley Railway to enjoy afternoon tea in the Pantiles at Tunbridge Wells.

In the foreground, the original Hurst Green Halt opened in 1907, just long enough for pull-push trains but also used in BR days by the front carriages of London services. It was replaced in 1961 by the new halt on the far side of the road bridge, having full-length platforms.

The parting of the ways at Hurst Green as class H tank No. 31544 propels its pull-push set on to the Hever line. Straight ahead leads to Lingfield, Dormans and East Grinstead. In LBSCR days, there were Inner Circle trains to Brighton via Horsted Keynes and Haywards Heath. There was also an Outer Circle service to Brighton via Lewes and either Eridge or Sheffield Park. None was a full circle, they were enterprising Victorian arcs. Let us alight at East Grinstead for a trip on the Bluebell line to take lunch at Sheffield Park.

Between Hurst Green and Edenbridge Town, Little Browns tunnel passes under the old SER main line to Tonbridge. It creates a pointed arch, an ellipse and a glimpse of winter trees.

Part 1 of

'Down the line to Oxted'

appeared in Issue 6 of 'Southern Times'

Class L 4-4-0 No. 31781 approaches Crowhurst Junction North on the spur from the old SER main line from Tonbridge. Selsdon to Crowhurst Junction was also a useful SER connection in emergencies, providing some of the many possible route permutations between London and the Kent Coast. Perhaps I will invent a board game, 'All Stations to the Seaside'? *John J Smith, 1961.*

Lingfield and Dormans were somewhat neglected for good photos of steam. Here is a rare shot of Dormans with a green DEMU in the Down platform when the author commuted to Forest Row for a short while. *Alan Postlethwaite, 1963.*

On the day we were preparing Part 2 of 'Down the line to Oxted' for inclusion in this issue, we received an email from Howard Read, Station Manager, Oxted Line, 1989 - 1993.

Mr Read comments, 'Having worked on the Oxted line it was good to see an article and photos many of which I had not seen before. I look forward to Part 2.'

He also adds, 'Just a few additions and clarifications which may be of interest.

'Page 54 Map - Sanderstead Station is between Selsdon and Riddlesdown

'Page 56 - The line under the left hand arch (Down Relief) did not become reversible until 1 June 1958 when a crossover (CV 27) between the up and down branch was provided. Until that time up Oxted line trains joined the Up Through at the south end of South Croydon (3rd line from left). They could until 1984 cross to Up Local line (far right line) by the crossover at the north end of the station (just visible in photo). The line under the left hand arch became a down line again (Down Slow) on 7 April 1984 as part of Brighton line resignalling. The 2nd line from the left then became reversible.

'Page 58 - The Oxted line platforms at Selsdon reopened on 1 March 1919 and were used by a few services until they closed on 14 June 1959. Platforms on the Woodside line reopened in 1935 upon electrification, closing in 1983.

'Page 59 lower photo - Train is crossing Riddlesdown Viaduct.

Page 61 upper photo - Photo is looking towards Oxted so train is from Lingfield.'

Oxted viaduct. Opened in 1881 it carried the railway over what is now the A25 road and the River Eden. This sepia image likely dates from the early uyears of the 20th century.

Civil Defence Exercise
Brighton Kemp Town

In 1949 the Government established the Civil Defence Corps. These were organised groups based around the country and intended to take local control of an area in the event of a national emergency. At the time this was principally seen as covering the threat of a nuclear attack coming from the Eastern Block countries but it was also intended to deal with more 'routine' emergencies including a major accident.

By 1956 some 330,000 personnel were involved around the UK who could be called to assist the civilian authorities, fire, police, ambulance etc, if required. The Corps was stood down in 1968.

Before this date however, regular exercises were held to test mobility and organisation, including one at Brighton Kemp Town on 28 September 1958, intended to simulate a major accident between road and rail. As such valuable experience could be learned by all those involved.

Gerald Daniels was on hand on the day and recorded these brief images.

The day started with the arrival of the train to be involved in the 'accident' hauled by C2X No. 32449. Details of the exact scenario are not available but it appears a collision of some sort was envisaged with persons trapped.

As matters progressed so persons were freed from their confinement - those wearing 'boaters' were from the private Roedean school and are believed to have been participants; note too in the lower view on the opposite page, how the roof of the bus has also been cut - some doors from the one of the railway carriages have also been removed.

Images Gerald Daniels / Transport Treasury.

Stephen Townroe's
Colour Archive
Mr Bulleid's Pacifics

For this instalment from the Townroe colour archive we feature the 'big uns', Mr Bulleid's pacifics.

As a mechanical engineer charged with ensuring he always had sufficient motive power available for both regular and additional duties, Mr Townroe freely admitted he was not always a fan of the Bulleid breed - certainly that is in their original form. This preference was certainly nothing against Mr Bulleid himself, but instead the unpredictable performance of the design: brilliant one day but the next day and with the same crew, lacklustre and only just able to maintain the schedule. Of course there were exceptions, one No. 34102 *Lapford,* which still in original form in the latter years of steam continued to be rostered to the heavy inter-regional passenger workings as a proven and reliable machine. Conversely a rebuilt engine did not necessarily mean a guaranteed performance, examples such as Nos. 34043 *Combe Martin* and 34045 *Ottery St Mary*, both early casualties due to consistent poor reliability. With no members of the Merchant Navy class based at Eastleigh, but instead seen 'visiting' and when of course ex works, it would be difficult to draw comparisons between individual engines of this class but no doubt similar criteria applied.

Turning now to the images in this section, some may have been seen before but their interest and rarity certainly warrants a repeat.

In both the accompanying views we have No. 35024 later named *East Asiatic Company* depicted with variations to the then standard BR Blue livery. Opposite is how the engine appeared with horizontal red bands, from 12 February 1949 until just 2 March 1949, after which the red bands were replaced with the black and white seen below. The below view shows the engine after a further works visit on 29 April when the wheels were painted black and a black 'splash skirt' added, the latter running the length of the engine and tender. Only three Merchant Navy class engines failed to be painted in blue, Nos. 35011, 35014 and 35023, No. 35024 also the first of the class to be repainted in what would then become the standard green livery in June 1951.

Considering the short time No. 35024 was in the livery seen opposite, this may well be the only colour image of the engine during this three week time span.

Both photographs were taken at Eastleigh.

Opposite top : No. s21C5 *Canadian Pacific* reversing out of the works in full Southern livery but with the addition of 'British railways' on the tender. The image was taken in 1948 and so may well be when it was first fitted with a mechanical stoker - see page 48.

Opposite bottom: Likely around the same time - allowing for the vauguries of contemporary colour film, we see the same engine this time alongside the Eastleigh coaling stage. When new, the high sided tenders of the Merchant Navy class collided with the side of the mechanical coaling plants; such as that at Eastleigh and modifications had to be made.

Above: Two 'Light Pacifics', again ex works and displaying different colour schemes - No. 34022 *Exmoor* (malachite) and No. 34064 *Fighter Command* (apple green), both ex-works although why Eastleigh should choose to paint engines in different colours at the same time is not clear. Ahead is Z No. 30956 and T9 No. 30119 (malachite). The restored T3 just creeps into the view on the right hand side.

Below: No. 34016 *Bodmin* on a different occasion and again ex-works sometime in 1948. Aside from the 's' prefix and tender lettering, the engine is in almost complete Southern livery.

Above: No. 35005 *Canadian Pacific* during its time running with a mechanical stoker, seen here at Andover Junction. (The line to the right heads to Andover Town and Romsey.) There were several separate time periods when trials were run in this form, the first from Eastleigh from 22 March 1948 until 2 April 1948 after which the engine re-entered works for adjustments. The second set of trials were again initially from Eastleigh before the engine was sent to Nine Elms for work on main line duties, including the 'ACE', and which continued until 25 October 1949 when the engine again entered works. This was for a scheduled heavy-intermediate repair but also to be prepared for trials at Rugby. Working re-commenced on 18 February until 26 February when the engine ran to Willesden en-route to Rugby. Trials here were on the stationary plant and concluded on 15 March after which the engine returned to the Southern Region for testing with the LMR Mobile Testing Unit between Battersea and Salisbury - which is probably when the engine was photographed. Comparison tests were then made with the stoker removed and a recourse to conventional hand firing. The mechanical stoker was refitted in the spring of 1950 and a final series of tests made from 17 November 1950. The engine reverted to conventional firing in April 1951. In conclusion most crews liked the arrangement - fireman no doubt pleased to be absolved of their normal labour - but control of the fire was more difficult and in consequence blowing off was more frequent whilst greater quantities of dust were created.

Opposite top: No. 35015 *Rotterdam Lloyd* waiting departure from Bournemouth West with the Up 'Bournemouth Belle' in 1951. Due to its length, when departure time comes the train will be started by a flag rather than with the conventional starting signal; this because the engine is standing on the track circuit ahead of the signal meaning the signal could not be cleared.

Opposite bottom: West of Exeter, No. 34004 *Yeovil* and note the extra long smoke deflectors, is in charge of the Up 'ACE' near Otterham in 1954.

Next time: Engines in and out of Works.

Similar treatment for No. 34003 *Plymouth* in September 1957. By now the new BR totem is applied to the tender.

No. 35013 *Blue Funnel*, ex works at Eastleigh and unusually out-shopped facing west instead of east. This was the third member of the class to be rebuilt and one of six so modified in 1956; photographed on 14 May of that year.

Above: The first rebuild was No. 35018 *British India Line*, out shopped from Eastleigh in the form seen on 9 February 1956 and after initial local trials and necessary minor adjustments, was despatched light to Nine Elms on 12 February for inspection by the Chairman of the BRB, Sir Brian Robertson, at Waterloo on 13 February. The engine is seen here against the stops of Platform 15 on 13 February and clearly attracting some admiring glances. Beauty is indeed in the eye of the beholder and whilst the original type were without doubt impressive, this was as much due their sheer bulk as much as their unusual appearance. In rebuilt form there was not a little similarity to the 'Standard' pacifics types especially with the raised footplating and design of smoke deflectors. No 35018 was destined to be unique amongst the rebuilds in the route taken by the pipe work on the left hand side, whilst the red painted front axle, just seen here and more clearly in the view opposite top, was not perpetuated.

Opposite top: Seen a short time earlier, wending its way to Waterloo ready for the VIP's. No doubt the crew were instructed to only have the engine in light steam although it will be noted there is also not a wisp of a steam leak from anywhere - totally contrary to how the class appeared a decade later!

Opposite bottom: Following rebuilding, a series of trials involving sister engine No. 35020 *Bibby Line* were carried out between Salisbury and Exeter Central. No. 35020 was the second of the class to be rebuilt although in April 1956, and as will be seen overleaf, at this stage the tender of No. 35020 had not been modified to the form seen above with No. 35018. The cut down tender suited the rebuilds well. Here we see No. 35020 on the Up through line at Exeter Central waiting a return to Salisbury. Posed in front is the chief of the testing section from Swindon, Mr Sam Ell - the WR dynamometer car was being used for the tests.

No. 35020 *Bibby Line* with original high tender fitted to the class (the tender was later transferred to No. 35028, outside Salisbury shed in August 1956. The engine and dynamometer car, No. W7W, are stabled on a dead-end road outside the shed where there also happened to be a stores van. The latter not forming part of the test ensemble.

Top - Royal Train duty for No. 34048 *Crediton* at Weymouth, 29 April 1959.

Bottom - Equally important but not so much in the public eye, was the Nine Elms breakdown train arriving at Reading (Southern) in June 1954 behind No. 34009 *Lyme Regis* (the consist was there to deal with a recalcitrant S15.) Note the 'V' headcode is same the one later used for the funeral train of Sir Winston Churchill.

Opposite top: This time it is No. 34019 *Bideford* at Corfe Castle with a through working from Waterloo in August 1956.

Opposite bottom: We conclude the presentation in this issue with a grubby No. 21C4 *Cunard White Star* about to pass through Shawford station with the down 'Bournemouth Belle' in October 1949. The line on the right is the down goods loop from the DNS at Shawford Junction connecting into the down relief line just south of Shawford station. Although the DNS has been closed for several decades, the loop line is still in use today, connected directly into the down main line at what is still called Shawford Junction and today used as a passenger line.

From the Footplate

As we were unable to include 'From the Footplate' is Issue 6, we are delighted to present a selection of comments and additions for two issues.

We commence with the continuation of the letter from **Pawel Nowak** at the foot of **page 80, ST5.** "You may be amused that, following various unsuccessful property machinations by our Northern-based property department, I have ended up at the former Hither Green Locomotive Shed, of which the western half survives as a maintenance facility for track machines, as does the SR rail-post mounted clock, which features on countless photographs from the 1950s. My current 1990 office replaced the former three eastern side shed roads and the very prominent water tower, but otherwise the actual track layout is largely identical to its steam-age predecessor, apart from the relatively recent removal of the turntable and the lowering of the former coaling stage siding to the surrounding ground level. In my childhood period the place was inhabited by 'C' 'Q1' 'S15' and 'W' classes, not to mention the solitary 'King Arthur' 4-6-0 allocated to a peak-hour passenger turn from Cannon Street, but it was much later that I actually visited the Marshalling Yard in which I did my early freight training, now retaining a very small freight presence, but mainly a depot for Networkers and other more modern EMUs.

With regard to the location questions in 'Southern Times' I was completely flummoxed by the picture on Page 74 of issue No 1 showing the two berthing sidings with a 4-SUB in one and 4-EPB in the other. I'm confused by the signals because I can't find in my collection of diagrams or in my memory any pair of sidings with a 3-way junction signal on the approach to them in the manner shown. It most be somewhere within 20 miles of central London judging from the rolling stock and the inter-war housing to the right of the picture, but I still can't place it.

"I think I'm on slightly more solid ground in the case of the picture at the top of Page 75, with a typical 1932 twin-headed junction signal in the picture and a 6-PUL unit with headcode '5', denoting London Bridge - Brighton via Quarry Line avoiding Redhill. By coincidence, your issue No.2 has a review on Page 63 of the comprehensive signalling history by Chris Durrant of the southern half of the Brighton Main Line. Referring to the signalling diagrams therein, the candidate location that springs to mind is Earlswood station facing north, but the signalling scheme plan diagram on pages 242-243 suggests that the left-side signal head is 4-aspect and the Up through Line signal

head on the right is 3-aspect, which the photograph does not support. The other possible location is Three Bridges facing north, where the signal configuration on Page 180 matches the photograph more closely.

"Finally, the signal box interior photographs starting on Page 57 of Issue No. 2 bring back a lot of memories. The Southern Railway, like London Transport towards the end of the inter-war period was very 'conservative' in that once they found a way of controlling complex junctions from one often very large electro-mechanical interlocking (e.g. the 313-lever frame at London Bridge) they stuck to it, apart from the refinement of splitting a single very long frame into three electrically connected frames arranged in a semi-circle for better overall supervision in the case of Waterloo and Victoria Central.

"The very different Victoria Eastern was an earlier order and matches many installations on the Great Western. The main advantage is the closer spacing of the slides as compared to miniature levers, which makes for a shorter frame by virtue of the alternative upward and downward facing handles. The article correctly points out the absence of 'route setting' in these miniature lever frames - the main saving in terms of lever numbers is the absence of separate levers for facing point locks and separate distant signals. The only case where a single lever might control more than one successive signal would be in the case of a succession of 'Automatic' signals with no route setting function. To find early UK route setting one had to travel north to Thirsk and Northallerton. The LNER was very much in the lead in this respect and the post-war installations at Liverpool Street, Stratford and other nearby 1949-vintage boxes were outstanding examples of both the 'Entrance - Exit' and 'One Control Switch' formats which set all the points between any pair of adjacent signals. World War 2 has a lot to answer for here, as the extension of colour light signalling from Purley to Bricklayers Arms Junction and Battersea Park took the best part of 20 years, with much prodding from the Railway Inspectorate following the disastrous collisions at Battersea Park and South Croydon through misuse of the Sykes Lock and Block release key in fog. Almost certainly this pressure influenced the retention of miniature lever frames having the benefits of familiarity for installers and maintainers. Even on the 'progressive' former LNER, the size of the control area became controversial to the extent that the Doncaster installation was split between two boxes at opposite ends of the platforms with a very small reach beyond the immediate environs of the station, although the next major scheme at York reverted to the originally intended large control area principle. Whatever the ultimate plans on the Southern or Eastern regions in the 1940s, many boxes were never replaced with switch panels or miniature lever frames but adapted with a mixture of levers and switches and often the points continued to be worked mechanically and only the main line running signals were colour light and shunt signals were pulled by wires if close enough to the box.

"The Kent Coast electrifications and track remodellings of 1960-62 were the Southern's 'Great Leap Forward' to enthusiastic adoption of 'Entrance-Exit' panels and some 'One Control Switch' examples such as at Chislehurst. The continuing weakness in comparison to other parts of BR was its slowness in adopting the 4-digit train descriptions used elsewhere. This meant that descriptions were passed from box to box in a generalised form showing an approximate class ('Fast Pass', 'Semi Pass', 'Stopping Pass', 'Engines/Vans/Empties' and 'Freight') with an indication of the route by means of naming a major location on diverging route beyond the next box , not the final destination. The signalman had in effect to keep in the 'Magazine Train Describer' a sequence of incoming trains approaching him from the box next door and choose an appropriate moment to delete them from the incoming describer and send them forward in a edited form to the next box. The descriptions did not 'step up' on their own.

"Signalling, like many operating aspects on a busy railway breed strong local loyalties and some Southern staff mourned the replacement of familiar 2-digit EMU codes on newer generations of EMUs, just as many staff at Stratford in my day hated the removal of the 4-digit train describers from freight locomotives in particular."

Pawel continued shortly afterwards, "The historic MPD clock is appropriately stuck at 15:50 or so. I wonder if it's worth restoring for the locomotive depot's centenary, whenever it falls... Must suggest it to the engineering firm which now lease the relevant section of the site.

"In time immemorial, Charles Dickens' works were frequently published in instalments with the breaks falling in dramatic moments. I'm amused by being promoted to his august company in the midst of some comments on the Brighton Main Line! I realise you can't fit everything in.

"The name Gerald Daniels reminds me of a 1969 visit during my training to the 1920s London Bridge Signal Box (all 313 levers in one straight line, unlike the later Victoria Central and Waterloo, arranged in three electrically-linked sections). He was an Assistant Station Manager at London Bridge at the time and in his very informative explanation he and the Regulator on duty commented on the potential unreliability of one piece of point work (No 277, I think), a switch diamond crossing some distance east of the station on the South-Eastern Main Lines, where the Down Fast trains towards New Cross would cross the Up Slow tracks.

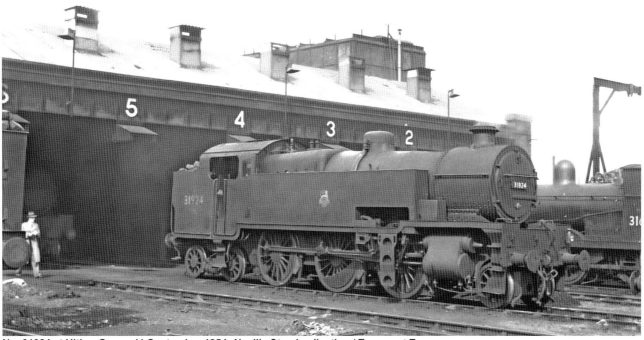

No. 31924 at Hither Green, 11 September 1954. *Neville Stead collection / Transport Treasury*

As if to order, it promptly failed during the conversation, so I had obviously jinxed it. A useful warning. The LNER 1949 layout at Stratford where I ended up a few years later was full of switch diamonds and they were equally troublesome. His Kempton Park photo from the 1950s makes me wonder whether anyone has ever published an article on the reversible working of the Down Line towards Shepperton on race days, where token instruments were apparently provided to permit incoming trains to be stacked on the Up Line waiting for the end of the racing while the odd train providing the remaining service back to Waterloo used the token working to return 'wrong-road' *(We are not aware of any such article - volunteers welcome...? Ed..*

From **Nick Stanbury** on **ST6** - on the topic of the Newhaven article. "I've just been scanning through ST6, another interesting issue. One very minor error noted on p17: the 'coast road' at Newhaven (now carried on the flyover) is the A259; the A27 is a few miles north of Newhaven, originally through Lewes but now by-passing it to the south."

Now from **Chris Knowles-Thomas** on **ST6**. "A couple of corrections, Page 35: No 30448 is not an S15, it is an N15 'King Arthur', *Sir Tristram.. Page 74,* 'IoW 'Terrier' W13 was originally 677, not 667 as stated. Consequently, as you state, it was renumbered 32677 when it re-entered mainland service. At first it retained the malachite green livery until, as you say, it was painted BR lined black in 1952."

From **Martin James**, starting first on Rusham Crossing Signal Box, **ST6**. "I worked in Rusham Box as a teenager - blocking trains on whilst the signalman sat outside in a deckchair !!! This block box was always in daily use as a block box and manned in two shifts - 6am to 2pm and 2pm to 10pm. It was closed at night - as was the crossing closed to road traffic at night."

Still from Martin and this time re Staines to Wokingham. "Virginia Water Coal Sidings; the track for these sidings is still in situ buried in the undergrowth - except where the new electrical substation has been built. The line after Virginia Water turns west-southwest … and not as stated. Since the building of Longcross Garden Village, for some years now Longcross has had a half-hourly service in both directions mornings and afternoons. The station here has also been refurbished in the last two years - with the exception of the Exmouth Junction Concrete Works footbridge. On page 31 the photo cation should read Weybridge to Waterloo - and not as stated. Waterloo to/from Reading services are a mixture of Class 458/5 and Class 450 EMUs, Ascot to Aldershot trains are always a single Class 450. For

A corner of the interior of the new signal box at Forest Hill in September 1950 showing the type of train describers referred to by Pawel. (The full interior image appeared in ST2.) .

some years now, Class 455s - and indeed Class 707s - rarely appear.

"I believe the photo on the back cover is of a Royal Train race special between Victoria and Epsom Downs, however, as it is not carrying the Royal Train Headcode, I suspect its an ECS (carrying the BR express passenger headcode)

"Finally, you mention AI in your editorial - please may I pass on a quote about AI. AI is like a small child. You don't know what it will do next. You also don't know whether it will turn out to be good or to be evil." (Martin - so true! Ed.)

From **Colin Martin** reference his images that appeared in **ST5.** "I must correct slightly one of your captions on page 61. No. 31623 is correctly propelling but not at Guildford. This would have been the early evening pick-up goods, about 18.45. Having arrived from the Haslemere direction and now being reversed from Farncombe West box into Godalming Old station yard (closed to passengers many years before). A regular spot to view this daily operation was from Manor Road footbridge, a short bike ride after tea.."

Finally for this issue, a most interest discourse from **John Bradbeer** re the editorial in **ST5**. "I guess that I won't be the only one to raise a question or two about the editorial in ST5 wondering what a continuing Southern Railway might have done, especially with what we now call the Withered Arm. It was not all a lost cause, even as the 1940s gave way to the 1950s. There was profitable china clay traffic on the Wenford Bridge line and profitable ball clay from Meeth/Petrockstow to Fremington, milk from Torrington, and, for a still steam operated SR, there was coal for the western part of the Western Section imported via Fremington. Perhaps even a diesel operated SR might have imported fuel oil at Fremington or Yelland (which was where a great deal of North Devon's oil and petroleum was imported).

"I know that historians hate counter factual histories (what ifs) but one important counter factual surely concerns the Transport Act which if not enacted, then the railway owned bus services would have continued as such. This is pertinent, as while the Traffic Commission regulated and effectively controlled competition between bus undertakings, Conservative government policy in the 1950s encouraged competition between nationalised rail and nationalised bus. One outcome was virtually no attempt to co ordinate rail and bus services and the idea that buses might call at railway stations to act as feeders or distributors was anathema. The one great exception was at Barnstaple Junction where the Southern National bus to Lynton started and finished its journeys, a result of pledge made by the SR when it closed the Lynton and Barnstaple Railway in 1935. Even so, the bus called at the station to suit the bus and not the train timetable and some connections were tight and in the evenings, the 15-00 from Waterloo (and the last down train) arrived at Barnstaple after the last bus to Lynton had gone."

The Editor reserves the right to shorten or reject correspondence without reason being given. The opinion of writers is welcome but may not coincide with that of the Editor or staff at Transport Treasury.

The rear of Redhill shed with the remains of a 4-4-0 of some sort. We know withdrawn and stored locos were often kept at the rear of the shed - as witness the 2-6-0 minus rods. However, the 4-4-0 appears to have been 'dismantled' rather than being cut up piecemeal; the boiler and firebox for example simply removed. Can anyone add anything further please?

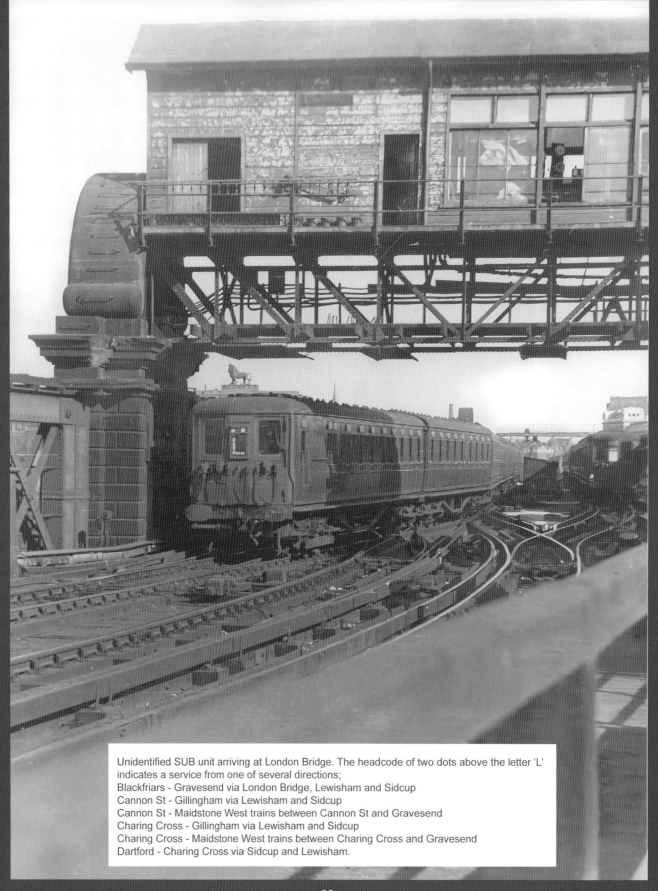

Unidentified SUB unit arriving at London Bridge. The headcode of two dots above the letter 'L' indicates a service from one of several directions;
Blackfriars - Gravesend via London Bridge, Lewisham and Sidcup
Cannon St - Gillingham via Lewisham and Sidcup
Cannon St - Maidstone West trains between Cannon St and Gravesend
Charing Cross - Gillingham via Lewisham and Sidcup
Charing Cross - Maidstone West trains between Charing Cross and Gravesend
Dartford - Charing Cross via Sidcup and Lewisham.

First Generation / Heritage 'EMUS'

Notwithstanding the Southern Railway has been a part electric railway for well over a century, the general dearth of EMU images compared with steam continues. Indeed it would probably be true to say that for every 50 or more steam images just one solitary EMU subject will appear and often it seems very much as an afterthought on the part of the photographer. A sad reality.

In recent years there has also been a trend to refer to the 1950s and 1960s DMUs and 'First generation' or 'Heritage'; in which case why should we not do the same for the Southern EMUs of the same period and earlier?

Assuming there are not too many dissenting voices this is indeed how we will generally refer to such units in the future - at which point it would well be appropriate to commence with some relevant images.

Top: This time we can be pretty certain of the set number, 4377. The service Gillingham or Fawkham - Blackfriars via Nunhead.

Bottom: 6-Pul set on a 'Victoria - Ore via the Quarry line and Eastbourne' service.

4-LAV No. 2955 at Victoria. One of the final
pair of sets built in 1939/40 and which differed
from earlier sets by having English Electric
instead of Metropolitan Vickers motors
although both were rated at the same 275hp.

Later 4-SUB set No. 4289. Headcode No
36 referred to as a Victoria - Beckenham
Junction via Streatham Hill and Crystal
Palace working.

Top: 6-PAN No. 3037 racing through Clapham Junction with a fast Victoria to Brighton service bypassing Redhill via the Quarry line.
Bottom: Sister set No. 3034 at the same location and with the same service as described on page 63.

Opposite: Western section working; 4-COR Set No. 3148 leading a Waterloo - Portsmouth semi-fast at Clapham Junction running via Worplesdon and scheduled to call at Havant. By the winter of 1964 this was one of two similar units incorporating a motor coach from a former 6-PUL unit.

Above: Guard Walker of Waterloo at Shepperton on 11 November 1958 alongside 4-Sub No. 4366 almost ready for the return working from the terminus.

No. 0365 is almost as built condition. The large splashes were decorative only and were not as might be expected additional water capacity, Built in June 1877, it received the duplicate number in Jul7 1896 and was withdrawn in October 1898.

The demise of William Beattie

Locomotive 4-4-0 No 365 (or as seen in the accompanying illustration duplicated as No 0365) was one of a class of 20 such engines of the '348' class built by Sharp, Stewart & Co. for the LSWR in 1877 to the design of William Beattie. They were also the largest tender engines built for the LSWR up to this time and unfortunately would prove to be similar failures as per the later large 4-6-0s built by Drummond some years later.

That a bigger engine was required by the railway is not in doubt, the principal expresses west of Salisbury frequently unable to keep to schedule due to ever increasing train weights. At that time 2-4-0s were in charge and to the design of W G Beattie's father, Joseph Beattie. The new engines, the '346' class - the designation taken from the number of the first of the type - was instead a new design which with the benefit of hindsight should really have been built as a single prototype before mass (20) production commenced.

Instead delivery from the manufacturer, Sharp Stewart ,was relatively quick after the order was placed in June 1877, and by March 1878 the first had arrived on South Western metals. After initial light engine trials revenue earning services commenced on semi-fast services to Southampton and Salisbury but problems quickly followed with valve and piston troubles. These were rectified at the makers expense, but were destined to be only the start of difficulties, with Beattie duly presenting a damming report on their manufacture to his Locomotive Committee in August of the same year.

This painted a picture of alleged defective manufacture and the use of poor quality materials, and in the absence of any contradicting evidence was initially accepted by the LSWR. Perhaps not unexpectedly the railway followed this with a demand that Sharp Stewart be compelled to put right their supposed failings, not surprisingly at their own cost.

What followed was a refusal by the manufacturers to accept any blame, at least until they had inspected all 20 engines at Nine Elms. This was agreed and similarly rapidly undertaken so that just two months later and by early October all had indeed been assessed.

What was found by Sharp Stewart totality contradicted Beattie's original allegations;

1 - The heating surface of the boiler was too small for the cylinder size.

2 - Poor steaming was attributable to a poor smokebox design.

3 - The firebox area was too small for an engine of that size.

4 - The piston and valve troubles were due to water becoming trapped.

5 - Inadequate lubrication was available to the valves.

6 - Unsteady riding was due to insufficient bogie side play.

As might well be expected, the makers refused to accept liability but did offer to modify the whole class (in what respects is not stated) for a very reasonable £240 per engine including transport costs to and from the LSWR. It was not taken up.

This report was similarly presented to the Locomotive Committee which cannot have been comfortable for Mr Beattie.

In the meanwhile Beattie, perhaps in effort to redeem his situation had three of the class taken into Nine Elms works for sundry (not detailed) modifications each also having a different lap distance, all also had new blast pipes. None made much difference.

At this stage Beattie was still convinced the issues were simple teething troubles, almost the final straw coming when the directors asked for a further update, which showed that on 12 December 1877 just four of the 20 were in service, the remainder either at or awaiting works. Eight days later Mr Beattie retired on the grounds of ill health, he had been in office for a few days over six years and at the time of his 'retirement' was just 36 years of age. He would live on for a further 40 years. The Locomotive Department of the LSWR remained in effect leaderless for only a short time, for on 20 January 1878 William Adams took charge having moved from a similar position on the Great Eastern Railway.

Under Adams tenure the class were altered both mechanically and aesthetically but they were never going to be a class destined for a particularly long life and only three would see service into the 20th century and then for just five years each. .

69

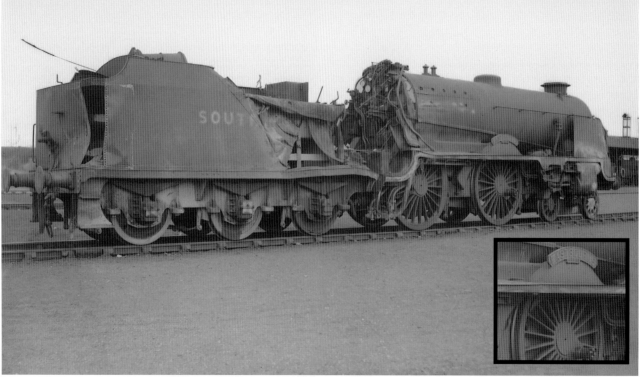

'St Lawrence', 'Eastbourne' and 'Ardingly'

The 'Schools' class entered wartime service as 40 engines scattered around the Eastern and Western sections of the Southern Railway. Intended primarily as a passenger design their curtailment of some passenger services upon the outbreak of WW2 in September 1939 led to a number being stored although all were subsequently returned to service.

The class were also unlucky when it came to damage caused either directly or indirectly by enemy action. This started with No. 934 *St Lawrence* just outside Cannon Street at 4.00 am on 11 May 1941.

An air raid had commenced at 3.55am with No. 934 at the time standing tender first on empty stock at Platform 8 *(another report states this to have been Platform 2)*. Incendiary bombs had already set the station roof alight causing burning debris to fall around the station. In an attempt to minimize the damage to rolling stock, arrangements were made to shunt a train standing in Platform 8 on to the river bridge, but it was first necessary to remove burning debris from the track and the roof of the train and extinguish a number of fires. All tracks, points and signal lights had also failed by this time. The move was assisted by H class 0-4-4T No. 1541. The task was nearly complete;

No. 934 coupled to No. 1541 pulling five loco hauled coaches and two electric sets to what was hoped to be relative safety away from the station and to the point where the ensemble was on the bridge across the River Thames. It was at that point that a string of high explosives fell, most in the river but one hit the cab of No. 934 before piercing the firebox and damaging the front of the tender. How the crew survived may only be guessed at, likewise the crew of the 'H' and other railwayman involved. Various items of rolling stock sustained damage, the blast carrying the body of an adjacent coach into the river and derailing three vans of a Newspaper Train previously on platform 6 which had likewise already been drawn out from the station. Most importantly the bridge remained standing. No 934 was taken to Eastleigh and repaired coming back into service on 27 August 1941. Driver Foote from No 934 was awarded the British Empire Medal for his gallantry.

Notwithstanding No. 934 having literally been hit by a bomb, another member of the class sustained greater damage two months later. This was No. 914 *Eastbourne*. On 13 June 1941 enemy action damaged an overbidge at New Cross and the engine ran in to the resultant debris causing it to become derailed. Fortunately speed at the time was low so there were

Opposite top; No. 934 in-situ just outside London Bridge, 'the morning after the night before'. The 'H' is coupled behind. Considering the damage is was indeed fortunate that the footplate crew survived.

Opposite bottom: Sister engine No. 914 arrived at Eastleigh for repair. The damage is similar to that suffered by No 934 but close examination will reveal subtle differences. Note also, various parts may have removed to allow for travel.

This page: No. 917 after its attack and stored pending repairs. From this angle the damage does not look too serious - but then view the next pages... .

no serious injuries although the damage to the left hand side of No. 914 was considerable and it spent six months, from June to December 1941, under repair at Eastleigh. What would emerge after repair was in effect almost a new engine as the repairs had included new frames, new cylinders, a replacement boiler and a new tank for the tender.

A third class member No. 917 *Ardingly* was damaged by enemy action on 11 August 1942. This was almost certainly at Deal where three bombs landed at 6.15 pm wrecking most of the station buildings, signalbox and bridges. The 3.15 pm Charing Cross to Ramsgate was standing on the Down line with No. 917 badly damaged Unfortunately the driver was killed and the fireman injured.

D L Bradley contradicts this slightly but on this occasion he may be awry. He states that on 21 August the same engine sustained a holed smokebox whilst at Ramsgate shed and in consequence of an attack by an enemy aircraft. The fireman was also injured himself by jumping from the cab and falling on to the track.

The accompanying illustration of No. 917 clearly shows far more damage than mere holes in the smokebox whilst in addition it is hardly conceivable that No. 917 might be damaged on 11 August and then repaired and be back in traffic again just 10 days later. The conclusion has to be a different engine was attacked at Ramsgate, class and number unknown.

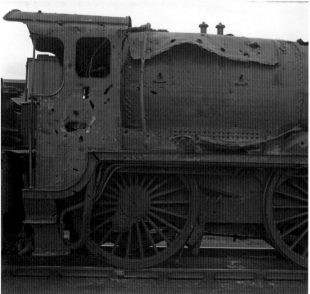

Various angles of No. 917 *Ardingly* after being attacked at deal on 11 August 1942 and prior to removal to Eastleigh for repair and likely taken at Deal. Note the position of the cranks on the driving wheels indicating that the coupling rods may well have been removed - ready for towing - in the position where the engine was photographed.

The views also confirms it is highly unlikely this engine could have been repaired in just 10 days and then attacked again at Ramsgate on 21 August.

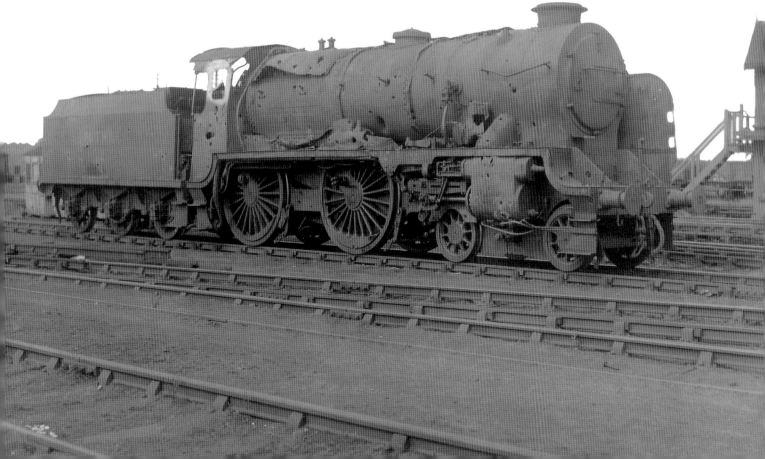

Southern Railway Floral Plate

The floral plate would have been used in one of the Southern Railway hotels. The plate would have been introduced in 1925/6. On the back is stamped Southern Railway, Chatham Section showing it would be from a hotel on the old South Eastern & Chatham Railway, such as Dover, Folkestone, Deal or Hythe.

Silver Plated Tankard.

The silver-plated tankard was made by Elkington in Birmingham. It has various marks, including '1 pint'. The use of a verification mark was compulsory on all vessels serving alcohol after the 1876 Weights and Measures act. The marks show that the tankard was assayed in 1897 in Birmingham *(lower right image)* and verified in Wimbledon. It is inscribed SWR Refreshment Department on the base. It would have been used either in a Railway owned hotel or at, say, Waterloo Station.

Earthenware Pot

A pot used in one of the Southern Railway Refreshment Rooms, operated by Frederick Hotels. It is believed that this pot contained some sort of reconstituted milk maybe used during the war.

Treasures from the Bluebell Railway Museum
Tony Hillman

The Bluebell Railway Museum China Cabinet

Like all Museums the Bluebell Museum at Sheffield Park has various cabinets for displaying artefacts. Some contain Signalling items, Permanent Way tools and equipment, Lamps, Staff items, Publicity material, etc. This article will list some of the items in the China Cabinet. It will quickly be seen that this cabinet contains more than just china, also including other refreshment car and hotel artefacts.

For the electrification of the railway line between London Victoria and Bognor Regis in 1938, 13 new four coach electric units, known as 4-BUF, were built by the Southern Railway at Eastleigh. One of the coaches was a buffet coach.

Fixed to the wall between the windows and either side of the connecting door between coaches were sets of six plaques depicting various items of food. The Museum is fortunate to have three of these plaques on display being those for Chicken, Fish and Vegetables. As well as the main picture other similar items of food are displayed around the perimeter.

The letters KG, inscribed within the picture are the initials of George Edward Kruger Gray, the designer of

these plaques. The other plaques showed Beef, Pork and Lamb. If any reader could provide any information as to the whereabouts of the other three, please contact the editor.

With new rolling stock being available these units were moved around the Southern network with the last units being scrapped in 1971.

SIX PLAQUES IN BRASS
designed by
R. KRUGER GRAY

A NEW FORM
OF DECORATION
IN THE BUFFET CARS

Chicken and Asparagus,
Bread Sauce (corn)
In the border, eggs & toast

Beef and Yorkshire Pudding
In border, horse radish and oxtail soup

Pork and Apple Sauce
In border, sausages and beans

Lamb Cutlets and
Mint Sauce
In border, sheep's hearts

Vegetables (cabbage, carrots, potatoes)
In border, radishes

Fish (hake, cod, sole)
In border, shrimps, cockles, mussels

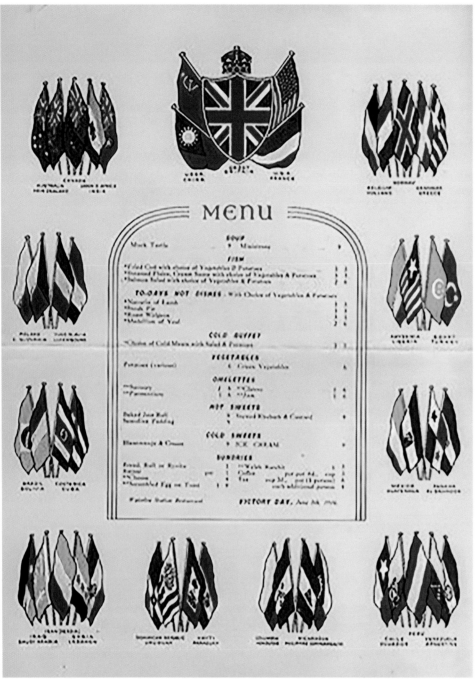

Victory Day Menu

Saturday 8 June 8 1946 was celebrated in the UK as Victory Day to commemorate the end of World War 2. The celebrations that took place in London consisted mainly of a military parade through the city and a night time fireworks display. Most British allies took part in the parade, including Belgium, Brazil, China, Czechoslovakia, France, Greece, Holland, Luxembourg and the United States.

The menu shows the special meal provided at Waterloo Station Restaurant and shows the flags of many of the British allies.

Next time:

A look through some of the Southern Railway paperwork held in the Archive, including the Southern Railway 1931 establishment census.

Hidden Names (the answers to the puzzle in the previous Southern Times)

The solutions to the hidden names in Issue 6 are as follows.

1. *Melisande*
2. *Wellington*
3. *Stevenson*
4. *Robert Blake*
5. *Trevose Head*
6. *Sir Galahad*
7. *Lord Anson*
8. *Morgan le Fay*
9. *Sir Lamorak*
10. *Tonbridge*

Many readers solved the "puzzle", and many also drew attention to the fact that "Stevenson" should be "Stephenson", and therefore the clue in this case was incorrect.

Southern Region in colour
Images by Ian Hemphill

Sidmouth approach in its final years of operation. The Ford Anglia 'Super' might even be said to be in the correct BR road vehicle livery!

With the takeover of the main line and branches west of Salisbury by the WR in 1963 so their stock began to be seen. Seaton now had a 14xx or 64xx and an auto coach to replace the M7s, whilst Sidmouth was operated by a diesel mechanical DMU.

The Yeovil Junction - Yeovil Town - Yeovil Pen Mill shuttle was also in the hands of a small 4-wheel railbus. Five of these smart little vehicles were built by AC cars, four for the WR and one for use in Scotland. They operated in the Yeovil area between 1964 and 1966 before moving elsewhere although all had been withdrawn by 1968.

Gaunt and empty, a desolate Yeovil Town engine shed. The adjacent Town station had closed to passengers in 1966 and to goods a year later. The site was subsequently levelled.

Moving east, another sight no longer possible is of a 'Terrier' waiting at Havant with the service to Hayling Island. The activities of the fireman (?) about to couple perhaps, seemingly of great interest to the schoolchildren. Immediately behind the engine is the fibreglass bodied coach S1000S.

A definite 1960s looking Gatwick Airport with a 4LAV. The train is a stopping Brighton service calling at Redhill.

We conclude this issue with a view of the level crossing and signal box at Uckfield. Sadly neither survive today although the station at least remains - albeit as a terminus. Perhaps one day it may be possible to venture south to Lewes again.